**A** is for Troy **A**ikman. The #1 pick in the 1989 NFL Draft, Aikman became the Cowboys' most-tenured quarterback of all time, making six Pro Bowls and winning three Super Bowls. His greatest moment came during Super Bowl XXVII, tossing four pinpoint touch-downs and winning Super Bowl MVP.

**B** is for **B**ob Lilly.
The leader of Dallas' vaunted
'Doomsday Defense' might
be the most loved athlete in
Cowboys history. In 1961,
'Mr. Cowboy' was the first
player the Cowboys ever
drafted. In 1975, he became
the first player inducted into
their esteemed Ring of Honor.

C is for Roger 'Captain Comeback' Staubach. Staubach's accolades could fill the pages of a book. He hurled the first-ever Hail Mary pass, led 23 game-winning drives for the Cowboys, and was awarded six Pro Bowl berths. But he truly cemented his status as a Dallas legend after winning the Cowboys their first Super Bowl back in 1972.

D is for Tony Dorsett. Dorsett's blazing speed and juke-you-out-of-your-shoes potential led to him being credited with the longest run in NFL history—a 99-yarder. He became an instant Cowboys legend during his rookie season, rushing for over 1,000 yards and helping guide Dallas to a Super Bowl victory.

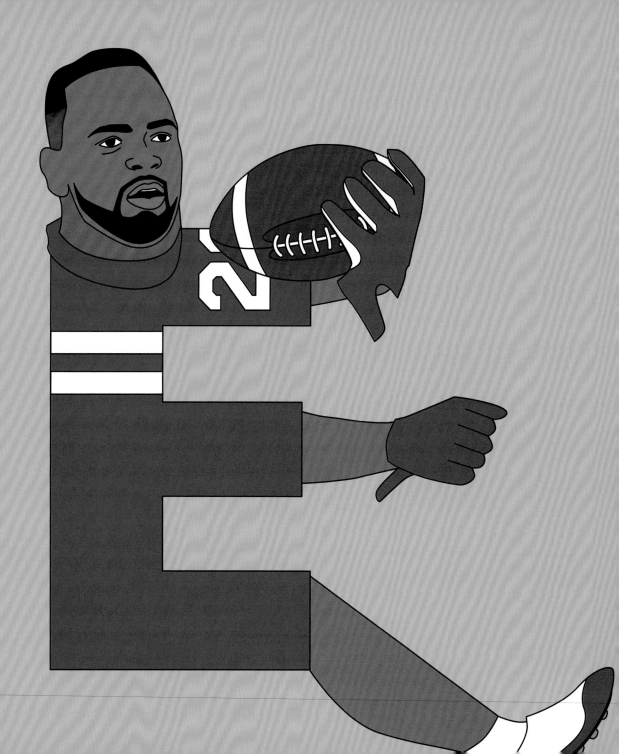

**E is for Emmitt Smith.**
The NFL's all-time leading rusher racked up a whopping 17,162 yards and 153 rushing touchdowns while playing for the Cowboys. During their dominant '90s 'Triplets' stretch, he was always Dallas' steadying force. Smith is the face of longevity and a true Cowboys legend.

**F** is for **F**lozell Adams. You've got to give credit to the big guys. In no sense is that truer than with the man Cowboys fans nicknamed 'The Hotel.' The toughest guy around, Adams missed only 14 games during his 12-year Cowboys career. Through extreme grit, he became an all-time legend in Dallas.

**G** is for Jason **G**arrett. Though he never won the 'Big One,' Cowboys fans will never forget 'The Clapper.' Garrett was often seen adamantly clapping on the sideline to encourage his players. By the time he and Dallas parted ways, he'd amassed 85 career wins—second-most in Cowboys history.

**H** is for Charles **Haley.**
Haley was mean—and that's
exactly what made him a
Cowboys legend. He hated
losing so much, he once
smashed his helmet through
a concrete wall after a loss.
Haley's passion eventually
paid off, as he helped the
Cowboys win three Super
Bowls during the '90s.

I is for Michael Irvin. His flashy personality, outrageous touchdown celebrations, and knack for finding the endzone made 'The Playmaker' a fan favorite in Dallas. His most legendary season came in 1995 when he accumulated franchise-record numbers in catches (111) and receiving yards (1,603).

**J** is for Jerry Jones.
As the owner of the Cowboys since 1989 and a three-time Super Bowl champion, Jones solidified his spot as a legend in Cowboys lore long ago. But his greatest achievement might be the creation of Dallas' AT&T Stadium, nick-named 'Jerry World' and widely regarded as America's greatest sporting venue.

**K** is for **K**yle Kosier. There are certain dudes you want fighting alongside you in the trenches, and Kosier was one of 'em. This calming, inspiring 6-foot-5 behemoth was loved by fans, coaches, and teammates alike. He started 80 hard-fought games in silver and blue.

**L is for Tom Landry.** 270 career wins, two-time Super Bowl champion, NFL Coach of the Year, and the innovative mind behind several defensive schemes that are still widely used in today's modern NFL. What more can you say? Landry is the epitome of a Dallas Cowboys legend.

**M** is for De**M**arcus Ware. 'Tank' had one goal: to terrorize the lives of opposing quarterbacks. And boy, he accomplished his goal. During his nine seasons in Dallas, Ware wreaked havoc upon any offense he faced. By the time he was done as a Cowboy, he'd stockpiled a staggering 117 sacks.

**N** is for Terence **N**ewman. Dallas drafted Newman fifth overall in the 2003 NFL Draft, then watched him live up to his potential over the next nine seasons. His most legendary moment came in 2009, when he helped the boys in blue and silver to an NFC Wild Card game win over their rival Philadelphia Eagles.

**O** is for Terrell **O**wens. Fans remember the acrobatic catches and outlandish celebrations. But what made T.O. a true Dallas legend was his tear-filled 2008 press conference in defense of Tony Romo. 'That's my quarterback,' Owens said. With tears in their eyes, Cowboys fans replied, 'Ours, too.'

**P** is for Dak **P**rescott.
Dak's numbers are truly out of this world: over 22,000 passing yards, 143 touch-downs, and a single-season, franchise-record 37 touch-down passes—all during his first six seasons. Dallas fans love this Texas legend, and they would quite literally run through a brick wall for him.

**Q** is for Dan **Q**uinn. Though his tenure in Dallas has been short, Quinn is already adored by Cowboys fans. Lauded for his loyalty, this Cowboy Defensive Coordinator could've secured any head coaching job he wanted following the 2021 season. Instead, he turned them all down and returned to Dallas.

R is for Tony Romo.
That impeccable smile. Those dimples! But what made Romo a true Cowboys heart-throb was his unbelievable underdog story: From undrafted free agent and backup quarterback to a perennial starter, the Cowboys' all-time leader in touchdown passes is also a Texas legend.

**S** is for Deion **S**anders. 'Neon Deion' was known for talking trash and backing it up. After joining the Cowboys in 1995, he played a pivotal role in Dallas' winning Super Bowl XXX. With all the accolades, the legendary man also known as 'Prime Time' easily high-stepped his way into the hearts of Cowboys fans.

**T** is for Bill 'Tuna' Parcells. Big Tuna wasn't around for long, but his stint in Dallas sure was memorable. After several seasons of losing, Parcells helped the Cowboys return to the NFL Playoffs during his first season as Head Coach. Most notably, he's remembered for developing Tony Romo into a star quarterback.

U is for Randy 'Ugly Baby' Gregory. Young, talented, and ferocious, Randy Ugly Baby Gregory has been a fan favorite in Dallas since taking the field in 2015. He dominated opposing back-fields in 2018, amassing six sacks and pressuring quarterbacks every chance he got. The sky's the limit for Gregory.

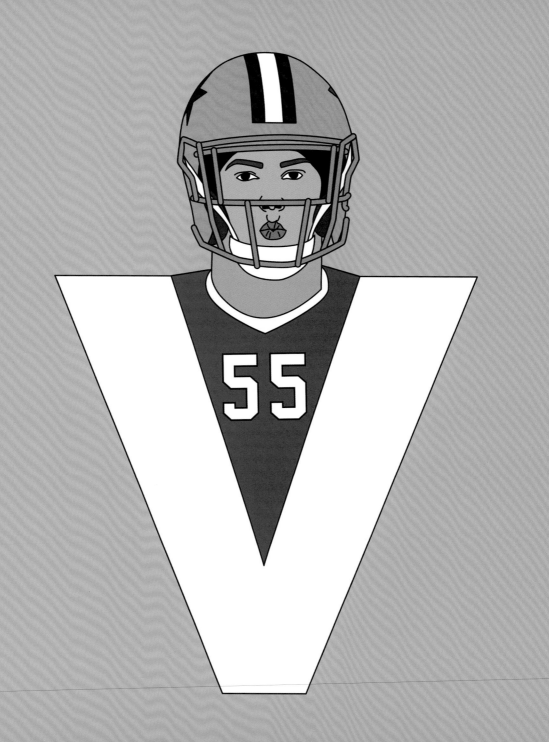

**V** is for Leighton **V**ander Esch. Vander Esch established himself as a Cowboys legend right off the bat. During his rookie season in 2018, he led the team with an eye-popping, bone-crushing 140 tackles. And in that year's NFL Play-offs, he contributed 10 more crucial tackles in a tight NFC Wild Card game win over the Seattle Seahawks.

**W** is for Jason **W**itten. The all-time leader in catches (1,215) and receiving yards (12,977) for the Cowboys is loved in Texas almost as much as barbecue. He played in nearly every game across 16 seasons for the silver and blue, establishing himself as the heart of the Cowboys squad and a true Dallas legend.

X is for Dez 'X' Bryant. Regarding his X celebration, Bryant had this to say: 'The meaning is to X out the negative. To beat the odds. To destroy adversity.' And that's exactly what Dez did as he established himself as Dallas' all-time leader in touchdown receptions with 73 over the course of eight legendary seasons.

**Y** is for The **Y**oung 'Lion,' Micah Parsons. Talk about instant impact. In his first year, Parsons led the Cowboys in sacks, won Defensive Rookie of the Year, and was already being mentioned as one of the best players in the NFL. Micah has many years left to play, but he's already a Cowboys legend.

**Z is for Zack Martin.**
The most bruising guard in the NFL plays for the Dallas Cowboys, and he goes by the name of Zachary Martin. He's played his entire career for Dallas and earned Pro Bowl honors in seven of his first eight seasons. By the time he hangs up his cleats, there's no doubting that Martin will be a Cowboys legend.

# The ever-expanding legendary library

**EXPLORE THESE LEGENDARY ALPHABETS & MORE AT WWW.ALPHABETLEGENDS.COM**

**COWBOYS LEGENDS ALPHABET**
www.alphabetlegends.com

Published by Alphabet Legends Pty Ltd in 2022
Created by Beck Feiner
Copyright © Alphabet Legends Pty Ltd 2022

Printed and bound in China.

9780645200171

**ALPHABET LEGENDS**